FINANCIAL AID OFFICERS

OFFICERS

**What They Do—
To You and For You**

ELEVENTH EDITION
DONALD MOORE

OCTAMERON
ASSOCIATES

Book and cover design by Bremmer & Goris Communications, Inc.

Address correspondence to:
Octameron Associates
PO Box 2748
Alexandria, VA 22301
703. 836. 5480 (voice)
703. 836. 5650 (fax)
www.octameron.com
info@octameron.com

ISBN 1-57509-059-7
PRINTED IN THE UNITED STATES OF AMERICA

CONTENTS

■■■■■■■■■■■■■■■■■■■■

INTRODUCTION

BY PAUL G. AASEN
DIRECTOR OF FINANCIAL AID,
GUSTAVUS ADOLPHUS COLLEGE

PAST-PRESIDENT,
NATIONAL ASSOCIATION OF STUDENT
FINANCIAL AID ADMINISTRATORS

A college president with whom I once worked often reminded me that as the school's financial aid officer (FAO), I had discretionary use of more funds than any other person on campus, including himself. I think this was his way of saying how important the FAO is to students, parents, and the institution.

Many people picture the FAO as the person with the "bucks"—someone you want to get to know. While it is true that the FAO makes financial aid awards to students, it is important to realize that the FAO has many other responsibilities. The FAO is an educator—one who helps others understand financial aid policies and procedures. The FAO is a manager—one who must make sure the office runs smoothly, that students are served on a timely basis, and that programs are administered according to the standards established by each source of aid funds. Lastly, the FAO is a counselor— one who advises students on financial planning, academic progress, and personal and/or family problems.

Through my experience, I have found that many students have misconceptions about financial aid. They make assumptions based on the experience of a friend or neighbor. They wonder why financial aid awards are not the same at all the schools to which they have applied. They lack information about their responsibility in assuming student loans. And they question whether they should or should not be considered independent. Most students find it difficult to make sense of all the forms and requests for additional information.

As a student, your ability to go to, or continue attending, the school that best meets your needs (not just financial), may be dependent on how well you understand the financial aid process. As a consumer, you have the right, and responsibility, to know how your aid eligibility is determined.

But how can you learn the "ins and outs" of financial aid without becoming an FAO yourself? Don Moore, the former FAO of SUNY-Oneonta, has come to your rescue. In writing this excellent booklet, he answers most of the questions you might have about financial aid—the questions we as aid officers must answer every day as we meet with students and parents. Questions like:

- How is my need determined?
- Will my aid be the same every year?
- Does a personal visit with the FAO help my chances?
- What happens if parents refuse to provide financial information?
- Will my grades in high school/college make a difference?
- Will financial aid really allow me to attend the school of my choice, even if it is a higher cost school?
- Why must "outside" scholarships be reported to the FAO?
- Can changes in my family's circumstances during the year (death, divorce, unemployment, etc.) be taken into consideration?

I strongly encourage you to read this booklet carefully. It will clarify the financial aid process which can help you both financially and personally. Mr. Moore, like most FAOs, is committed to helping students. He cares—we care—about you. Good luck in your search for more help.

A Summary of Don's Best Advice

1. If you are applying for aid, know the deadlines, and apply by those dates. Do not expect the aid administrator to change dates for you.

2. Make sure the applications are complete and accurate. People trying to make sense out of someone's financial statement must receive complete and accurate information.

3. If you are going to visit the college, make an appointment to speak with the financial aid administrator as well as the admission officer.

4. Keep records of all the material submitted to the college or processor so you have evidence of doing what you said you did.

CHAPTER 1
■■■■■■■■■■■■■■■■■■

A QUICK TRIP AROUND THE HORN

These Darn Forms

"Mr. Moore, do I have to fill these forms out every year?" This was the question I was asked most often at financial aid presentations before high school and parent groups. Unfortunately, I had to respond in the affirmative, knowing that the complexity of the forms (or a perception of their complexity) creates a barrier to many students and parents who just hate the hassle of working through all the "administrivia."

Actually, the number of applications a family must complete has declined over the years. Today, most families need only file the Free Application for Federal Student Aid (FAFSA) while others, if required by a college, will also have to file the College Scholarship Service's PROFILE or the college's own financial aid questionnaire. After that, the family sits on pins and needles awaiting the outcome.

A number of years ago I eliminated our college's financial aid questionnaire since it duplicated information I could glean from the FAFSA and I worried that its existence might discourage some students from the aid process by acting as an additional hurdle. Many colleges, however, continue to use their own financial aid questionnaire (or PROFILE) because they truly need more comprehensive family data in order to divvy up their own student aid resources. There is some consolation, though, in that PROFILE and the college questionnaires are usually fairly simple to fill out, once you've gathered the financial records necessary for the FAFSA.

Free Application for Federal Student Aid

All students seeking financial aid should file a FAFSA. It's free, and fairly easy to file. Currently, you have three options:

Paper FAFSA. Beginning in October or November, you may pick up a paper FAFSA in your high school guidance office. You complete it (after January 1) and (snail) mail it to the address given on the form.

FAFSA on the Web. You may also complete your FAFSA directly on the Web (www.fafsa.ed.gov). This electronic FAFSA includes on-line help and instructions, while internal edits help prevent errors and reduce rejections.

Renewal FAFSA. If you are a continuing student, you will receive a renewal FAFSA from the Federal Processor. It will come pre-printed with much of the data you submitted last year, making it much faster to complete. If you completed your last FAFSA on-line, you will receive a personal identification number (PIN) that allows you to access and complete your renewal FAFSA on-line, as well. Generally, students who receive financial aid in one year will receive this form beginning in mid-November for the next processing cycle.

PROFILE

The College Scholarship Service (CSS), in cooperation with select colleges across the country, has developed a service called PROFILE to help schools award their institutional scholarship funds. PROFILE registration information may be found in high school guidance offices. If any of your colleges require PROFILE, call CSS (800-778-6888) to get your packet of forms, customized with each of your school's financial aid questions. You, then, complete the forms and return them to CSS. CSS processes the data and sends the results back to you as well as to all the schools you identified. You may also complete PROFILE on-line at www.collegeboard.org.

Students must pay a fee to use PROFILE.

Because PROFILE may be submitted earlier than the FAFSA, financial aid officers can use the results to get a head start on awarding institutional scholarships and estimating aid packages. Generally, the packages they develop based on PROFILE are pretty accurate, but Uncle Sam still needs to have results from an official FAFSA before he will disburse any money from the student aid sources he controls.

In short, PROFILE is used mostly by colleges which have lots of their own scholarship funds to give out, not only to estimate student eligibility for federal aid, but also to decide which students should receive money from collegiate resources. Colleges with limited scholarship funds have less use for additional family data, and ask students to file only the FAFSA.

Colleges should indicate in their publications which forms they require.

It's January 1

When do you submit the FAFSA? Not before January 1. The processors won't accept forms before that date. How much later than January 1? It depends on the application deadline established by your colleges; you may have to complete and file a FAFSA as early as the first week in January for the school year that begins the next September. But, you ask, how can you complete this task when you have not done your taxes? And to compound the problem, when you have not received your W-2s (which often are not mailed until the last week of January)? Actually, it is not quite as bad as it seems. If you are required to complete a FAFSA early, you may estimate your income, taxes, and other calculations.

Estimating Your Income

Estimating your financial figures may be the only way for you to get your forms processed in time to be considered for all financial aid programs. But—and this is important—you must exercise caution when making estimates because later in the processing cycle, you may have to send the college a signed copy of your income tax form. The aid administrator will compare your estimates with the information on the tax form to determine the accuracy of the original figures. If your original estimate is within a (federally-sanctioned) tolerance range, your family is OK. You will not have to correct the information. If, however, the correct information exceeds the acceptable tolerance level, you may have to correct the original data.

The Tolerance Level

The Department of Education has developed tolerance levels to determine when it is necessary to reprocess your FAFSA. There is one tolerance level for ALL federal student aid programs. Here's how it works: FAOs must verify your Adjusted Gross Income, Untaxed Income, and US Income Taxes Paid. If the discrepancy between the amounts you submitted on your FAFSA and the amounts shown on your income tax documents exceeds $400, you must submit your data for correction.

	Original Data		**Verified Data**
Adjusted Gross Income	$45,000		$46,000
Untaxed Income	+ $300		+ $300
US Income Taxes Paid	- $5,000		- $5,600
Total	**$40,300**	**Total**	**$40,700**

Net Difference = $40,300 - $40,700 = $400. Correction not necessary.

As you can see, you must estimate very closely if you want to avoid error correction. Oftentimes, however, the college will recalculate all data prior to requesting a correction to determine if the discrepancies change the student's eligibility. If this recalculation does not affect student eligibility, the family may not be asked to make any corrections. If, on the other hand, it does affect eligibility, families must resubmit their data so their new eligibility may be officially calculated by the FAFSA processor. While this means an extra step, the familiy's first priority should always be to submit the FAFSA on time. If the family misses the college deadline, they may be completely eliminated from the campus-based aid programs, a fate much worse than having to correct a few errors. Another point of concern: At some colleges, if you don't receive aid your first year, you're unlikely to receive school-based aid for the duration of your program.

The Processor

After completing the FAFSA, the family submits it to the appropriate college or colleges via a processing agent. The processor is simply a middleman responsible for analyzing data, editing the forms for integrity, and reporting the data analysis to the family, the college, and other appropriate financial aid agencies such as your home state for state grants. Many families mistakenly assume that the processor awards funds to students when in actuality the processor simply provides a service; the college controls the money.

Once the processor receives the data, reviews it for integrity and consistency, and analyzes the data, it sends a hard copy of the form along with its analysis to all colleges indicated by the family. If the processor finds problems or errors in the data, it will request updates from the family, thus delaying the time it takes to get results to the college. It makes good sense for the family to answer all questions as accurately as possible.

The Student Aid Report (SAR)

About four weeks after submitting your FAFSA, you'll receive an acknowledgment from the processing service, called a Student Aid Report (SAR). The SAR contains a variety of useful information—including a figure indicating your Expected Family Contribution (EFC) to college costs, as well as the data upon which the EFC is based (presumably the data you originally provided). Review it all carefully to make sure you provided accurate information. If you filed a PROFILE, you will receive a separate acknowledgment for that form from the College Scholarship Service.

Meanwhile, Back at the Financial Aid Office

Remember, you're not the only one sending data to the financial aid office. Your form will join those from hundreds, even thousands, of other families. The financial aid office, if you can visualize it, is being flooded by torrents of paper. This is probably the most hectic time in the life of an aid administrator. From the one-person office to the largest university, aid administrators and counselors are busily reviewing thousands of FAFSAs. Obviously, in larger institutions much of the work is computerized and thus somewhat impersonal; while at the smaller schools, each form is actually read and reviewed by one of the professional staff. Quite often, in reviewing the material, an aid officer will seek additional information or clarification by sending a special request to the family. In this way, the college can make its awards using the most complete and accurate information possible.

This is also the time of year many parents and students call the financial aid office hoping to influence the award process. Aid officers dread this. Although FAOs will try to be as responsive and courteous as possible, callers should know that finding an individual student's folder, at this time, is like locating a needle in a haystack. Quite often, student folders are separated by "financial need," or "problems," or "date of receipt," or "continuing students," or some other factor, and searching for a file folder in this jungle becomes a near impossibility. Many families who call during this time probably think the office staff has gone on a South American junket when, in reality, the staff is sweating bullets looking for the file. There have been occasions when the staff, after exhausting all avenues and cul de sacs in a search, discovered that the family was calling the wrong school!

Award Policies

Long before the first FAFSA arrives in the office, the staff will have reviewed procedures for determining how they will distribute funds. Offices with multiple counselors must establish internal policies so each applicant receives consistent treatment. While some may think this seems like bureaucratic esoterica, it does have a significant impact on the applicant, for these policies ultimately determine who will receive what aid and, more importantly, who will not receive aid.

Clearly, the internal procedures at larger institutions will be more sophisticated and complex. They use computer-simulated class profiles to establish financial aid parameters. Conversely, at small institutions with one-person offices, the procedures will be less technological and more intuitive. In either case, the procedures must be written out and available to aid applicants so they may discern the method by which assistance is awarded.

Office procedures will probably detail such general items as how to distribute grant funds, what the expected work load of work-study students should be, how to fit loans into the financial aid package, and what size student expense budgets the college should allow.

The Student Expense Budget

The foundation of every student expense budget is the school's annual tuition costs; an amount which may range from $750 a year to over $25,000, depending on whether the school is a publicly-supported college or an independent, private college.

Added to tuition is the cost of campus housing. This charge covers the cost of an on-campus student room for the academic year and may be as high as $6,250. Since the student who lives on campus will have to eat somewhere, the college probably offers a board plan through the college dining service from which the student will have to purchase meals at a cost of $4,150 or so, depending on the type of plan and the number of meals it covers.

Beyond these "fixed" expenses will be other items such as books, fees, travel, and personal expenses; even the cost of a new computer (generally no more than $3,000). Books depend on the courses selected. Personal expenses, which include health insurance, laundry and medical costs, can vary greatly. If the student is handicapped, for instance, or has child care expenses, the personal expense item may be set very high. And transportation, of course, can include commuting to a nearby school or multiple round trips to a distant school. When the student puts all of these costs together, a fairly accurate picture of one year's college expenses will emerge.

Developing realistic student expense budgets is critical to selecting eligible aid recipients; for this budget (a.k.a., cost of college) is one of the two major components of the formula that determines financial need (the other being family contribution). Many colleges have multiple student expense budgets, depending on the variety of students enrolled at the college. Along with a standard undergraduate student budget for on-campus residents, there may be a commuter student budget, a graduate student budget, a married student budget, as well as budgets recognizing different curricular costs.

To illustrate this variety, look at the budgets for four categories of students at one California college:

Student Category	Budget
Single Student, Lives at Home	$12,270
Single Student, Lives in Dorm	16,670
Single Student, Lives in Own Apartment	17,800
Married Student, Child Care Expenses	22,870

Quite often, the budget is a shock to the prospective student and family since it can range from $5,000 to $35,000+ per year. When these costs are considered over a four year period, the educational experience often becomes the second largest single expense ever incurred by the student's family, with only a home costing more. Clearly, then, the family must consider its educational objectives and strategies very carefully.

Financial Need

Wake up financial aid officers in the middle of the night and they'll say, "Need." It's the word most frequently used by FAOs, and one of the functions performed by the financial aid office is to separate those who demonstrate need from those who do not.

How do you demonstrate need? Generally, after establishing the appropriate student budgets, the FAO subtracts the family contribution from that budget. The resulting figure is the student's financial need.

Expected Family Contribution

And what constitutes expected family contribution? It's a combination of (1) a parental contribution from income and assets (2) a student contribution from assets and (3) a student contribution from income. All of these calculations are based on information you provide on the FAFSA.

The EFC figure often shocks families. In fact many families dispute the size of their contribution, considering it too high for their circumstances and in relationship to the family's other expenses. Such families perceive their need differently than the aid office. In Chapter 5 we talk about what families can do when such a perception gap exists.

A real world example will help establish the connection between "student expense budget" (or college costs), "family contribution"—and its three components—and "financial need." The Jones family is expected to contribute $7,000 to a college education that costs $12,000 at State U., and $25,000 at Private C. That family has a financial need of $5,000 to cover expenses ($12,000 minus $7,000) at State U. and $18,000 at Private C. ($25,000 minus $7,000). As the cost of college changes, so does the relative need of the student.

Awarding Aid

At one time, most colleges were able to support a "need-blind" admission program. Under this policy, admission decisions were based entirely on the ability of the student to succeed academically at that college. In other words, the student's one worry was to get accepted. The college took care of the student's financial need. In that golden age of admission, or rather, financial aid, students truly had freedom of choice in school selection.

Today, however, that has changed. Even the most expensive, most selective, and wealthiest colleges are having second thoughts about "need-blind" admission and are reviewing the applicant's ability to pay before offering admission. The entire applicant pool is not subject to such a review, only borderline applicants who barely meet admission criteria, and "tail-end" applicants whose forms come in after most of the available financial assistance was distributed to the "quicker" applicants.

The plain fact is that most colleges simply lack the resources to meet every student's full level of determined financial need. Colleges, like any other organization, must maximize their finances, and the move away from "need-blind" admission is a response to the current resource squeeze.

Responding to FAFSAs may be as simple as ranking all students from high need to low need and awarding funds until they are exhausted and then notifying those who will not receive aid of the unhappy results. Most colleges, however, attempt to recognize both need and ability. They have developed ranking methods that consider a combination of factors like need, academic ability, and special talent, and then award funds to students who score high using these various elements.

While need will determine the total amount of aid the student can receive, the academic ability or talent may determine the composition of the financial aid package.

Given similar levels of need, for example, the more gifted student may have more grant or work funds than loan funds. So, while the amount of money in the students' packages may be equal, the more "desirable" student may receive a more favorable mix of funds. Review the following packages awarded to two students, each of whose net financial need is $5,300.

	Student A	Student B
Net Need	5,300	5,300
Work Funds	1,300	1,100
Loans	2,200	1,100
Grants/Scholarships	1,800	3,100

Clearly the aid packages have been structured so the more talented Student B receives $1,300 more in grant funds than the less-promising Student A.

Enrollment Management

While the above scenario is fairly simple, the fact is many colleges practice something more complex, which they call "Enrollment Management." In essence, these colleges study the close connection between recruitment, admission, and retention to enroll and retain the best class they can. To do this, they refine their financial aid packaging policies to get the most bang for the buck. Colleges may segment various groups of students to determine the best way to entice them and keep them enrolled. There may be packaging strategies for freshmen, upperclassmen, students with special skills, students at different income levels, and students with different performance levels on standardized tests.

By using these techniques, colleges hope they will be successful in enrolling the kinds of students they want as well as keeping them after they enroll. But it also means students may find considerable variations in their awards. For example, the same student may be a highly sought after recruit at one college, and a "who cares?" at another. The aid package at each school may reflect this difference.

Accept or Reject

Once the FAO develops a package, he or she gives it to the student to review, and then accept, or decline. This aid package contains specific information concerning the award and an explanation of the steps the student must now follow. There may also be a deadline date by which the student must notify the college of acceptance or refusal. Heed this deadline! If you miss it, the college might cancel the award. If there are compelling reasons why you cannot respond by the deadline, you should contact the aid office, explain the circumstances, and request an extension. The college may be willing to grant an extra week or so, but probably not much longer.

Conceivably, the offered aid package might contain less money than expected or no money from a particular, preferred program (like work-study). If the information accompanying the award is not clear in explaining the "size" and "mix" of the package, contact the aid office for an explanation. In fact, by doing so, you may bring new information to the attention of the aid officer who might then increase or change the package.

Here We Go Again

After negotiating this round of seemingly confusing paperwork, the student can relax for the next six to eight months before they must repeat the process again for the next academic year. In most cases, every financial aid program requires annual applications with appropriate supporting documents. It pays to stay on top of deadline dates. The good news? Most students find the filing process gets easier each year.

But remember: Every year, family situations may change and so will aid eligibility. Income may go up or down; the number of family members in college may increase or decrease; and the eligibility formula may change. It is very possible for the student to be ineligible for aid one year and eligible the next, and it is also possible to lose aid because of these changes.

Some Tips

- Be sure you let the aid office know of your interest in a particular aid program such as work-study. An aid office ignorant of your preferences may exclude that program from your package.

- Do not expect to receive identical packages—either in size or composition—from year to year. Expect change and learn to cope with it.

- Do not expect to receive identical packages—either in size or composition—from school to school. Your package will be based on need, the school's resources, and the degree to which the school wants you to enroll.

- Make sure you follow all instructions contained in the aid package. To do otherwise might jeopardize your entire award. You certainly don't want to lose a lucrative award because of some foolish error.

- Make an appointment with the aid administrator and ask about the office's packaging philosophy.

A Summary of Don's Best Advice (cont'd)

5. Use certified mail to make sure all documents reach the proper destination on time and that you have evidence of this.

6. Do not wait for your tax forms to be completed before you file. You are allowed to make "reasonable" estimates.

7. Make certain to respond to any and all inquiries and requests as quickly as possible.

CHAPTER 2
■■■■■■■■■■■■■■■■■■■■

FREE APPLICATION FOR
FEDERAL STUDENT AID

In the first chapter, I sketched the aid process from the time you submit the Free Application for Federal Student Aid (FAFSA) to the time you receive the award letter. We will now retrace our steps, but at a slower speed and with more detail. This chapter is devoted to explaining the FAFSA (with a few words about PROFILE)..

Don't Leave Anything Blank

Always complete the FAFSA as fully as possible. FAOs are not mind readers. They need an explanation for each blank you leave. Don't hesitate to enter "0" or "None" or "N/A" if a question does not apply. This care may save the extra work of answering an inquiry from the college.

If a question or two seems confusing, ask your guidance counselor for assistance or, failing that, call the college. If the question still proves troublesome, explain yourself in a letter to the financial aid officer. Let's now start with a review of the application.

Step One: Student Information

The first group of questions covers demographic information about the student—name, address, social security number, date of birth, phone number, driver's license number, citizenship status, and marital status,

The next section asks about the student's educational plans, his or her expected student status (full-time, three-quarter-time, half-time or part-time), the highest level of education completed by the student's mother and father, the student's state of legal residence and the types of aid for which he or she wants to be considered (for example, loans and/or work-study). To maximize your chances for receiving aid, you should indicate a willingness to accept loans and work-study. You can always change your mind later.

If you're male, age 18-25, and not yet registered with the Selective Service, you may also use this section to register. (In most instances, male students must be registered to receive federal student aid.)

Step Two: Student Income and Assets

This section is a little trickier. It asks about the student's income and assets. Married students must include their spouse's income and assets, as well. I'll say more about recording financial data later in this chapter.

Step Three: Dependent vs. Independent

Step Three of the FAFSA addresses student dependency status. Students seeking to be treated as independent from their parents for financial aid purposes must satisfy one of the following criteria:

1. Be twenty-four years old by December 31 of the award year.
2. Be a graduate or professional student during the award year.
3. Be married (or separated).
4. Have legal dependents other than a spouse who currently receive more than half their support from you.
5. Be an orphan or a ward of the court.
6. Be a veteran of the U.S. Armed Forces.

Students who meet one of these criteria may apply for federal financial aid as *Independent*, while those who do not will be required to include parental data on the FAFSA.

Students may also be judged independent by the financial aid officer based on documented unusual circumstances. Since some students try to use "independence" to enhance eligibility for assistance, many colleges are tightening their institutional rules and making it more difficult for phony "independent" students to slip through.

The FAFSA also notes that graduate health profession students may be required to complete this parental information section even though they are (by definition) independent students.

Step Four: Parental Information

Dependent students must provide information about their parents' income and assets, as well as their parents' marital status, number of household members, and state of legal residence, tax filing status, and the age of the older parent. If the parents are divorced or separated, include only the financial data on the parent with whom the student lives for the greater part of the twelve months preceding the date of the application. If that parent has remarried, the student must include that stepparent's income and asset data as well.

Step Five: Independent Students Only

Independent students must answer two quick questions about the number of people in their household, and the number of household members who will be enrolled in college during the upcoming school year.

Step Six: Names of Colleges

Students may list up to six colleges that are to receive their processed data. Students must also indicate their housing plans (on-campus, off-campus or with parent) at each school, so aid officers may better determine their cost of attendance. If possible, record each school's federal school code. You'll find these codes on-line (www.fafsa.ed.gov) or in your high school guidance office. If you cannot locate the correct school code, be careful to record the school's complete name, address, city, state and zip. The processor won't know whether "U. of M." refers to the University of Michigan or Maryland, or whether "University of California" refers to the branch in Los Angeles or Davis.

If you are applying to more than six schools, use the FAFSA for your top six picks (or the schools with the earliest deadlines). When you receive the results, you can add additional schools.

Step Seven: Sign and Date the Form

Finally, students (and parents) must sign and date the form. In doing so, they certify that (if requested) they will provide information (for example, a copy of their tax return) to verify any recorded data. They also declare that they are not in default on any federal student loans, and promise to use any federal student aid for educational purposes only.

If the form was completed by someone outside your immediate family, that person must sign and date the form, as well. There is nothing wrong with getting help with your FAFSA, however, the Department of Education wants to know—that way it can clear up innocent misunderstandings, as well as detect patterns of fraud and abuse.

Income and Assets

In completing the parent and student income sections, refer to the IRS's definition for items like "AGI"—Adjusted Gross Income. Also, use your tax return if available. You must indicate whether your income data is based on a completed tax form or an estimate. There is no penalty for estimating. It does not affect your eligibility for aid unless a later comparison with the tax form shows it to be outside the tolerance levels described in Chapter 1.

The number of exemptions, adjusted gross income, and US income tax paid are lifted directly from the income tax form. The FAFSA even gives you the exact line reference numbers for the 1040, 1040A, or 1040EZ depending on your tax filing status. "Tax paid" means actual federal tax owed and paid, not the amount of tax withheld on a W-2.

It is important to indicate whether earned income is from two workers or only one. Where there are two workers, the family receives an additional allowance that helps increase the applicant's eligibility for aid. This allowance also applies to a single parent household when that parent has earnings from work.

Families must include all other income like untaxed Social Security benefits, welfare benefits (excluding food stamps), tax exempt interest income, deductible IRA and/or Keogh payments, child support received, worker's compensation, and in-kind income. Generally, families have no difficulty with income questions, but they are bothered by having to include in-kind income like housing or food allowances provided by an employer. The FAFSA's instructions will clarify the reporting of in-kind income.

Families may exclude a few items from their reported income and taxes— for example, child support paid, taxable work-study earnings, Hope and Lifetime Learning Tax Credits.

Your Assets

Asset questions seem to give families the most difficulty, because most people think the "net value" of their assets will eliminate them from aid consideration. Families must remember, they receive an asset protection allowance to shelter some of their assets and even then must contribute only a small percentage of the balance. The net value of an asset, by the way, is calculated by subtracting any indebtedness from its current value.

Your assets include the balance of your checking and savings accounts (as of the date you sign the form), as well as all of your current investments, including trust funds, mutual funds, money market funds, CDs, stocks, bonds, Education IRAs, and real estate. You may *exclude* the value of your primary residence as well as the value of any prepaid tuition plans, life insurance or retirement funds (e.g., annuities, IRAs and pension funds).

Unusual Circumstances

With proper care, you should have no trouble filing the FAFSA on time. Besides, if you have unusual or unique situations that do not seem to fit any category of the application, you can speak to the FAO about them later.

For example, if a divorce or separation is not reflected in the tax figures, the FAO might be persuaded to prorate the family's income and assets. If a divorce or separation is reflected in the tax figures, the parent with whom the student generally lives is the one who should complete the application. Some colleges will request information on the "other" parent and may expect some contribution from that parent as well.

How about severe illness? If you send a full explanation with supporting data, the FAO might consider the unusual expenses and job loss associated with the illness in estimating the student's aid eligibility.

While the FAO has discretion in reworking some of the data on the application, there must be sufficient documentation to allow a recalculation. Quite often, the FAO will need a special letter or statement from the family, or a doctor, or maybe even a lawyer to consider the effects of the special circumstances. Where it is clear that the family situation has been drastically affected by an unexpected calamity, the FAO will try to help as much as possible. But if it is a matter of blowing smoke, the FAO may be less than sympathetic or even downright uncooperative.

The Crying Towel

Some families simply live above their means. Then, as a child gets ready for college, they find themselves unprepared to finance those costs and unwilling to change their lifestyle. Instead, they want someone else to assume the responsibility of college costs for their child. Families who want to shift the payment burden to others will not find the FAO very sympathetic to their request. Simply put, some families want others to pay their way through tax dollars or personal donations so they can keep on living their own life without sacrifices that accompany the financing of a college education. Quite often, the college will take a very strong stand on this point, making it clear who should shoulder the burden of college expenses.

The Previous-Year Rule

A family's aid eligibility is usually based on the calendar year prior to the student's matriculation because this "previous year" is the last one for which information can be validated. Families often fear this will work against them. For example, a family that experienced considerable overtime employment in the previous year may feel this earnings peak will distort its contribution to college costs and cause considerable financial difficulties in future years in which overtime earnings will not be readily available. The same holds true for the small businessman who had one banner year but whose business has since slacked off.

While this may sound a little rigid, I have never seen a family estimate projected income to be higher than previous income. Besides, if the next year's income does prove to be lower than last's, that will be taken into consideration for the upcoming academic year. Note how a fluctuating income is considered in aid eligibility calculations.

Calendar Year	Income	Eligibility Year
2000	$51,500	2001-2002
2001	$42,000	2002-2003
2002	$57,000	2003-2004
2003	$39,000	2004-2005

Students vs. Parents

Because of the money crunch, colleges are taking stronger positions when it comes to allowing exceptions to standard procedures. Each year, a few students, having locked horns with their parents, often over issues totally unrelated to college attendance, seek assistance from the FAO by trying to apply for aid without using parent income information. Occasionally the FAO will relent, but only in the most exceptional of circumstances. Colleges will almost always insist that parents complete the FAFSA or the student will not be considered for assistance. As things stand today, the student will be unable to secure significant assistance on his or her own.

A Word About PROFILE

Profile asks the same basic questions as the FAFSA, however, schools may supplement this core form with hundreds of additional questions, depending on their institutional needs. For example, they may ask about the value of primary and secondary vehicles, life insurance annuities, tax-deferred pension plans (like 401(k)s), itemized deductions, child care expenses, and consumer debts.

If you're applying to one of the 250-plus schools that require PROFILE, you may register via the College Board, www.collegeboard.org.

A Summary of Don's Best Advice (cont'd)

8. Call before you visit the college to make sure the person you want to visit will be available.

9. Read all materials from the financial aid office carefully. If you have questions, ask the people who should know, not your neighbor or your uncle who has a friend in the business.

CHAPTER 3
■■■■■■■■■■■■■■■■■■

THE PROCESSOR

The Central Processing System

The US Department of Education, in combination with Congress, through various committees and focus groups, determines the formula to calculate Expected Family Contribution from the data families provide on the FAFSA. It also determines how to use each data item and what weight to assign to each in the calculation.

Once this is done, these decisions are translated into a computer program and passed along to the Central Processing System (CPS). The CPS is simply a private company that contracts with the Department of Education to evaluate a family's financial data and calculate the corresponding EFC.

Whether the family submits its data electronically or via a paper application, all of the data goes through one computing system. At this time, the CPS performs a number of checks to help ensure the accuracy of the data and the eligibility of the students. For example, it matches your data with the Social Security Administration, the Selective Service, and the Immigration and Naturalization Service, since, in addition to having financial need, all aid applicants must have a valid Social Security number, residency status, and (men of a certain age) must be registered for the draft.

In addition to these matches, the CPS performs a thorough audit, much like that used by the IRS, to check the mathematical accuracy of the data as well as the internal consistency of the information. For example, if a couple reports they are divorced, but provides income for both spouses, the CPS highlights that inconsistency and asks the family to review the information and make whatever corrections are necessary.

After all of these processes have taken place, the CPS calculates a family's EFC and sends them a Student Aid Report. The Central Processor also sends the information to the designated colleges either electronically (computer to computer) or via computer tape. Most state grant agencies have also contracted with the CPS to receive data which these state agencies then use to award state grant money.

The CPS does not make any awards. It is only a processing agency. It is the responsibility of each college (or state) to use the data to make whatever awards are appropriate given its applicant pool and available funds.

Acknowledgment

Within six weeks (Uncle Sam says four weeks) of sending off the FAFSA, the family will get a Student Aid Report (SAR) from the processor. Check the information to be sure it is correct. If there are errors, make the corrections, sign the form, and return it to the processor. In approximately two to four weeks, the processor will return the corrected SAR to you.

If six weeks pass and you receive no acknowledgment, contact the processor, using the directions in your FAFSA instruction book.

The Processor and the College

About the time this is happening, the college will also receive its data report from the processor. Generally, the aid office will review the information to make sure it is complete and accurate. If the FAO has questions concerning the information, he or she will request additional documentation from the family which usually includes a copy of the latest income tax return. Once the aid administrator is satisfied with the information, he or she will estimate student eligibility for federal and state grants, determine the "net need" of the student (using the student expense budget as the base) and, finally, make appropriate awards. Also at this time, the administrator will decide which students are not going to receive aid from the college. They will transmit these decisions to the student as quickly as possible.

In Summary

The processors play an important role in the field of financial aid. It should be clear, however, that while they "help" determine eligibility, they do not make decisions about who will receive the assistance.

In many cases, aid officers accept the information provided by the processors without making any significant changes to family contribution schedules or other numerical data. When, however, FAOs, in their professional judgment, believe the information should be changed, they will recalculate the raw data and make appropriate awards (for better or for worse) based on their revisions. This occurs most often where institutional, rather than governmental, funds are involved. In these instances, the FAO often has more complete data about you at his or her disposal, since you've likely been asked to file the more comprehensive PROFILE or the institution's own aid application.

CHAPTER 4

■■■■■■■■■■■■■■■■■■■■

THE FAO GOES TO WORK

The financial aid award process is ultimately the culmination of all of the plans and calculations aid administrators have made not only during the preceding year but during their entire professional lives. Awarding aid is both science and art. In part, it is based on empirical data, and, in part, it is influenced by the administrator's intuitive sense.

The Student Expense Budget

Calculating student expense budgets can be as simple as updating prior budgets to reflect inflation and any increase in fixed costs (tuition, room, board, etc.), or the process can be as complicated as drawing up sample expenditures for various students who reflect the different demographics of the student body.

Quite often, the process entails a little of both. In some years, the FAO may reevaluate the entire budget using such means as sampling students, examining bookstore costs, questioning local landlords, and considering national trends like inflation and other consumer costs. Depending on the size of the institution, the nature of the college, the college location, and the mix of students, the FAO may use several budgets when making awards. For example, there may be in-state and out-of-state undergraduate student budgets, a graduate student budget, an off-campus student budget, or a commuter student budget.

In fact, I have known some colleges to have a score or more of these student budgets. Consequently, when making awards, aid administrators must be sure they put students into the proper budget category so they calculate the students' financial need (and aid eligibility) correctly.

The following items should be included in every budget breakdown:
- Tuition and all required college fees
- Health Insurance, if applicable
- Books and Supplies for an academic year
- Room and Board for an academic year

CHAPTER 5

■■■■■■■■■■■■■■■■■■■

THE AWARD LETTER

Issued by the FAO, the Award Letter is a financial statement covering a single academic year. It describes not only what financial assistance the student may receive, but also how much will be expected from the family.

Identifying the Student Expense Budget

Typically, an Award Letter will show the student expense budget against which the FAO calculated the student's eligibility for assistance. The budget should reflect all costs reasonably associated with attendance—tuition, fees, books, room, board, personal expenses, and transportation. Typically, transportation costs include from two to four roundtrips home. If any of these categories are excluded from the budget, contact the financial aid office to determine whether it made an error or whether the college has a policy against funding some of the non-fixed costs.

Family Contribution, I

After identifying the student expense budget, the Award Letter will pinpoint the family's expected financial contribution. The Letter may even itemize a separate contribution from parental income and assets and student income and assets. For example, students are expected to contribute 50% of their after tax income above a fixed amount (currently, 50% of everything over $2,250) towards the cost of education. Unless students can show reason why this amount should be excluded from their contribution (e.g., it went to support their family), each college will make this portion of student earnings part of the family contribution.

Family Contribution, II

If the school has its own aid application, or requires families to file a PROFILE, it may calculate a second EFC using an "Institutional Methodology." While a school cannot use this value to determine your eligibility for federal student aid, it may adjust your EFC before awarding any of its own money. Typically, a school might increase the contribution from parental assets to reflect any home equity, or increase the contribution from student earnings to reflect some minimum amount, like $700 or $1200. They might also decrease the contribution from income to include an allowance for elementary and secondary tuition expenses.

The Student's Need

Now comes the exciting part of the Award Letter. By subtracting the family contribution from the student budget, the college calculates the student's financial need which, through a combination of resources, it will try to meet.

First, the FAO estimates the student's eligibility for a Pell Grant and a state grant and the probable size of these awards. It is, of course, to the student's advantage to receive as much grant assistance as possible.

Next, the college add in the amounts of other aid the student expects to receive. This might include Veterans benefits or an outside scholarship. If the student has considerable need remaining after these steps, the FAO can begin distributing the federal money controlled by the college through the three campus-based programs, Perkins Loans, Work-Study, and Supplementary Educational Opportunity Grants. Should the student still have unmet need, the college, can either dip into its own endowed scholarship programs or suggest that the student secure a Stafford Loan.

Different schools have different methods for closing the "need gap." Most start with "self-help" which consists of loans and work programs and then proceed to grant assistance, with grants from federal and state funds as well as the college's own resources. A few schools do the reverse, although nearly 100% of all colleges now include loans as part of every student aid package (up from 66% in 1988).

But no matter what the method, each package contains some combination of the same elements—grants and scholarships, loans, and work opportunities—which may or may not fully meet the student's need.

The Student's Response

After reviewing the Award Letter and any accompanying documents, the student must decide whether to accept or decline the award.

It's possible the family may be disappointed with various aspects of the package. Perhaps the parental contribution seems too high. Maybe the student contribution from earnings and assets seems too great. The package may seem too heavy on loans and too light on grants. Although the student may have expressed an interest in work-study, the package may not contain any funds for employment. Worst of all, the family may be left with a wide open, unmet gap between total costs and total resources. What can you do about all of this?

Negotiating with the FAO

First, let me remind you that honey catches more flies than vinegar. Quite often, families who are disappointed with the award letter will demand that the FAO take some action to rectify the presumed shortcoming. They force an unpleasant encounter that leaves both parties upset and the issue unresolved.

The best way to bring your concerns to the attention of the FAO is by telephone or letter. I recommend telephone—they seem to work better than letters to identify and solve problems. Letters sometimes raise new questions which may then lead to a series of letters between parties, causing delays and adding to the frustrations.

Quite often, disgruntled families suggest visiting the aid office to discuss their situation in detail and in private. My reaction: The visit will be no better than a telephone call, but more costly. I often suggest to parents that if they have nothing new to add to the financial picture, a visit will probably be a waste of their time. To have significant changes made in the Award Letter, the family will probably have to demonstrate financial hardships like unemployment, costly medical expenses, or other equally serious (and unpleasant) events over which the family has no control. If the family wants to do nothing more than recount how the ravages of inflation have demolished its pocketbook, the FAO is unlikely to adjust the award.

If the initial phone call reveals a change in the family situation, the aid office will expect the family to report these changes in writing and document them as fully and accurately as possible. Documentation might include reports from third parties such as physicians, lawyers, or counselors; it might consist of bills or receipts; or it could take the form of reports from insurance companies or the like. While some might find this requirement a bit intrusive, when families are asking to have their situation judged differently, it's only fair that they prove their case.

Tuition Remission

Of course, tighter aid budgets also mean more restrictive judgments by the financial aid officer who must strike a delicate balance between granting all exceptions and granting none. Generally, private colleges are more flexible in adjusting aid packages than public universities, which can often negate the fact that their attendance costs are considerably higher. In the preceding chapter, I discussed the greater freedom in governance and fund dispensation that private colleges enjoy. Here I'd like to mention their greatest advantage, an additional tool denied public universities called *"tuition remission."* Quite simply, a private college can just lower the amount of tuition it will charge that particular student. No money changes hands. The college does not give the student a check. It simply decides to take less money. Some of my colleagues call this "funny money."

Outside Scholarships

Students must notify the college if they receive outside financial assistance such as help from local scholarship agencies or philanthropic organizations. If FAOs learn about such assistance before preparing an Award Letter, they will incorporate this information into the aid package. If FAOs learn about it after issuing an Award Letter, they will have to restructure the package by lowering the assistance provided by the college and adding in the new aid. From the college's perspective, this adjustment makes good sense. It allows the college to distribute its money as fairly and widely as possible. Many parents, however, feel this restructuring is grossly unfair because the amount of aid the student receives remains unchanged (and the amount they pay out of their own pockets also remains unchanged). "How do we benefit from this scholarship?" parents may ask.

A family that feels this way might try to convince the college to have part of the loan funds contained in the Award Letter replaced by the outside scholarship. In Revised Aid Package #1, the family did not talk to the FAO and the outside scholarship was used to reduce the student's College Grant. In Revised Aid Package #2, the family persuaded the financial aid officer to use the scholarship to eliminate the student's Stafford loan. While this may not be as good as lowering the amount the family has to pay, it at least lowers the amount the family has to repay.

	Initial Package	Revised Package 1	Revised Package 2
Student Expense Budget	$9,000	$9,000	$9,000
Family Contribution	$4,000	$4,000	$4,000
Outside Scholarship	$0	$1,000	$1,000
College Grants	$2,000	$1,000	$2,000
Work Program	$1,000	$1,000	$1,000
Perkins Loan	$1,000	$1,000	$1,000
Stafford Loan	$1,000	$1,000	$0

Any time Uncle Sam offers financial assistance, he's going to issue rules for how the money is awarded and how long recipients may continue to receive the award. This is true whether one is building federally-subsidized roads, or administering a federal student aid program. Consequently, programs that may otherwise work well are tied up by the need to safeguard public funds from unscrupulous administrators trying to make a fast buck, or applicants trying to get more than they deserve. In other words, the government must generate reams of rules and regulations to protect all the honest program administrators from the 1% who are dishonest rip-off artists. While the rules are necessary, they sometimes make it difficult to help those truly in need. When this happens, the aid administrator becomes as frustrated as the family but has no choice other than to turn the applicant away. Thus, while FAOs try to operate programs within the letter and spirit of the law, some families see them only as people withholding needed help rather than as people helping the needy. There is considerable irony in the fact that FAOs, who entered a helping profession, should be perceived by so many as ogres unwilling or incapable of helping poor students and parents.

Frankly, I know no one in the profession who wants this reputation, but we all live with it, hoping someone will come along to help change the way we are viewed. Much of the FAO's work is tied up in rules, regulations and money. The more limited the resources, the more limited the ways the administrator can address unusual or unique situations. In many cases, funds are so limited the administrator cannot help even the high-need students. In some institutions, the financial aid office is forced to develop distribution formulas that spread limited dollars in ways that don't address the full need of its applicants. As a result, no applicant receives enough funds, and all must either sacrifice more to come up with a larger family contribution, or borrow from additional loan sources.

It is in this context that the aid administrator must explain the operation of the financial aid program to concerned and upset parents who, pressured by imminent college bills, are unwilling to accept what they are being told. Many parents feel others are receiving money they should be getting and that the administrator should rectify the situation.

What these families do not realize is the zero-sum nature of the financial aid budget game: If one family is added to the aid population, the administrator must then exclude another family. It is a difficult choice to make. It means administrators must have empirical data to justify their decisions. FAOs will nearly always offer assistance to the family which can demonstrate its need using concrete data before they will help a family which is not able to prove any need.

Professional Judgment

The Higher Education Act provides the financial aid officer with some flexibility regarding the use of professional judgment. But, the Act does not allocate additional funds with which to support wholesale reductions in family contributions. So this flexibility becomes a double-edged sword. On one hand, the FAO is able to make local decisions, but on the other, no additional funds have been allocated to support these decisions.

FAOs are most likely to use their discretionary authority to assist families when the need analysis system seems to break down, however, FAOs will still require documentation regarding a family's inability to contribute to college costs before making that decision. If families believe they have extenuating circumstances that affect their level of family contribution, they must notify the financial aid office in such a way that the FAO can make a sound judgment.

Farewell to Access and Choice

Access and choice, once the buzzwords of student financial assistance, are being abandoned because the funds to effect this are no longer available. With sources of student aid having stabilized or diminished, families are being told they must become more self-reliant and lower their expectations of receiving much assistance. Many are being priced out of the college of their choice.

Families frustrated by this situation might do well to think of the aid administrator who is becoming catatonic by the tug of war between families and dollars. FAOs are there to help, but have seen their role degenerate from a partner in the process of student financial assistance to the person who checks tax forms, asks embarrassing questions, and takes money away from people. Financial aid professionals abhor this characterization but these tasks are more and more necessary if funds are to go to the most needy and not the most creative. Because of limited funds, because of higher living costs, because of increasing college costs, more and more families are using questionable tactics in filling out their forms. This means aid administrators must ask for even more data, and examine it closely to verify financial need.

The policeman's role, while never written into the job description, has become a major component. Families must somehow put this into context when they visit the financial aid office. The willingness to help is there, the interest in the student is there, the commitment to honesty and integrity is there, but often the financial aid officer is thrown into an adversarial position and may not seem to have the enthusiasm families anticipate.

What to Expect from the FAO

Families should not expect the aid administrator to tell them on-the-spot how much, if any, aid they will receive. Families should not expect the aid administrator to change information without careful and proper documentation. And families should not expect the aid administrator to adjust financial aid deadlines for them.

What families should expect is fair and equitable treatment from the college. They should expect a timely response to their application. They should expect a reasonable answer to their questions.

In summary, do not hesitate to contact the aid administrator at the college you plan to attend. Do not hesitate to ask questions about your situation or where you stand in relation to other applicants. Do not hesitate to ask other reasonable questions. By doing this, you will receive a good idea of what to expect from the college. Remember: Aid administrators will help as many students as possible in the fairest way possible with the funds they have at their disposal. But nothing can be done with money that is not available.

A Summary of Don's Best Advice (cont'd)

10. Understand the terms and conditions of all assistance offered. Make sure the offer is a solid commitment and not just an estimate or preliminary assessment of eligibility.

11. If you have been dealing with an intermediary like a coach, department head, or other college official who seems to be offering some kind of financial assistance, make sure the intermediary has the authority to do that. Check with the financial aid office.

12. Inform the financial aid office of any outside scholarships, grants, or other assistance you will be receiving.

13. Review the student expense budget carefully to make sure it contains all the reasonable costs you will incur for your education.

14. Resubmit your FAFSA each year.

15. When in doubt, ask.

COMPARING AID PACKAGES

	College A	College B	College C
Cost	_____	_____	_____
EFC			
Parents	_____	_____	_____
Student	_____	_____	_____
Total	_____	_____	_____
Need	_____	_____	_____
Financial Assistance			
Gift Aid	_____	_____	_____
	_____	_____	_____
Total (1)	_____	_____	_____
Student Loans	_____	_____	_____
	_____	_____	_____
Total (2)	_____	_____	_____
Parent Loans	_____	_____	_____
	_____	_____	_____
Total (3)	_____	_____	_____
Work-Study	_____	_____	_____
Total Aid (1+2+3)	_____	_____	_____
Gap	_____	_____	_____
(Cost - EFC - Total Aid)			
Total Gift Aid	_____	_____	_____
Total Loans	_____	_____	_____
Total Work	_____	_____	_____

College Planning Guides from Octameron

Don't Miss Out: The Ambitious Student's Guide to Financial Aid **$10.00**

Hailed as the top consumer guide to student aid, *Don't Miss Out* covers scholarships, loans, and personal finance strategies. It will save readers hundreds, if not thousands of dollars in college costs.

The A's and B's of Academic Scholarships **$9.00**

Money for being bright! This book describes 100,000 awards offered by nearly 1200 colleges. Best of all, most of these (which must be used at the sponsoring school) are not based on financial need.

Loans and Grants from Uncle Sam **$6.00**

Increase your eligibility for federal student aid. This guide describes it all—the aid application process as well as loans and grants for students, parents and health professionals.

SAT Savvy: Last Minute Tips and Strategies **$6.00**

Nervous about the SAT? Whether you took a test prep course or are relying on innate ability, SAT Savvy contains all the tips you need to boost your confidence and your scores.

Majoring in Success: Building Your Career While Still in College **$8.00**

Take advantage of internships, work-study, volunteerism and cooperative education to offset college costs, connect with future employers, build a strong resume, prepare for job interviews, and much more.

Financial Aid Officers: What They Do—To You and For You **$5.00**

Should you accept your award package as offered? Can you request it be changed, or increased? Knowledgeable dealings with FAOs can result in more money. This book shows you how.

Behind the Scenes: An Inside Look at the College Admission Process **$6.00**

Ed Wall, former Dean of Admission at Amherst College, offers sage advice and detailed profiles of successful applicants. An invaluable view from inside on how the selection process really works.

Do It Write: How to Prepare a Great College Application **$6.00**

Personalize your essays so they stand out from the crowd. Author Gary Ripple is the former Admission Director at Lafayette College and the College of William and Mary

College Match: A Blueprint for Choosing the Best School for You **$8.00**

Author Steve Antonoff combines dozens of easy-to-use worksheets with lots of practical advice to make sure you find schools that meet your needs and your preferences.

Campus Pursuit: Making the Most of the Visit and Interview **$5.00**

Nervous about your interview? In his companion book to *Do-It Write*, Gary Ripple gives advice that will help you shine, as well as show you how to maximize the benefits of a campus visit.

College.edu: On-Line Resources for the Cyber-Savvy Student **$9.00**

Lost in Cyberspace? *College.edu* takes you to hundreds of useful sites on admission and financial aid, giving you Internet tips and warnings along the way.

Campus Daze: Easing the Transition from High School to College **$6.00**

Learn what to expect during your first year of college and how to succeed starting on Day One. Author George Gibbs is the former Dean of Admission and Freshmen at Muhlenberg College.

Financial Aid FinAncer: Expert Answers to College Financing Questions **$6.00**

Learn how special family circumstances impact on student aid.

The Winning Edge: The Student-Athlete's Guide to College Sports **$6.00**

It's all here. Scholarship opportunities. NCAA rules and regulations. Advice from coaches. Sample athletic resumes. Strategies, timetables, and worksheets—all to help you take your sport to college!

College Savings R$_x$: Investment Prescriptions for a Healthy College Fund **$6.00**

Includes both short- and long-term college planning strategies.

The Best 200 Colleges for the Real World **$15.00**

Get in. Get out. Get a job. Written by Michael P. Viollt, President of Robert Morris College (IL), this book is for the new student-consumer and evaluates colleges based on convenience, quality and cost.

Calculating Expected Family Contribution (EFC) Software **$42.00**

Estimate how much you will be expected to pay for college. This Windows 95/98 compatible CD-Rom software holds data on hundreds of families and let's you analyze different income and asset scenarios.

Ordering Information

Send orders to: Octameron Associates, PO Box 2748, Alexandria, VA 22301, or contact us at: 703-836-5480 (voice), 703-836-5650 (fax), or www.ThinkTuition.com (Internet). **Postage and Handling:** Please include $3.00 for the first publication, $1.00 for each additional, to a maximum of $5.00 per order. **Method of Payment:** Payment must accompany order. We accept checks, money orders, American Express, Visa and MasterCard. If ordering by credit card, please include the card number and its expiration date.